CONTENTS

What is puberty?

Puberty is a series of changes that happen to you as you grow up. Over several years, the changes of puberty help you turn from a child into an adult.

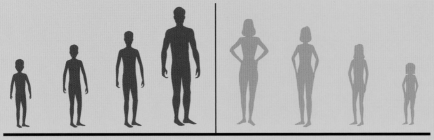

Ten-year-old boy → Adult man   Adult woman ← Ten-year-old girl

When does it happen?

Puberty is a gradual process – and the changes don't all happen at the same time. For most people, it will begin somewhere between the ages of eight and 14, and carry on for several years until the person is 16 or 17. However, some of the changes can happen earlier or later. And puberty often starts slightly later for boys than it does for girls.

What kinds of changes?

Puberty involves several different types of changes, so it can feel as if it's taking over your whole life!

Physical changes

The most noticeable changes are physical, or to do with your body.
- You get taller and grow hair in new places.
- Girls grow breasts and start having periods.
- Boys get a deeper voice and broader shoulders.

I feel fed up today.

I don't know why I'm sad.

Emotional changes

At the same time, you may experience new feelings.
- Puberty can cause mood changes, making you feel irritable, angry or weepy.
- Puberty in itself can make you feel alarmed, worried or confused, especially if you're not sure what's happening.
- Feelings of excitement, friendship and happiness can be intense, too.

Puberty
AND
GROWING UP

Anna Claybourne

W
FRANKLIN WATTS

9580000082655

Franklin Watts
Published in Great Britain in 2018 by The Watts Publishing Group

Credits
Series editor: Sarah Peutrill
Editor: Sarah Ridley
Art director: Peter Scoulding
Series design and illustrations: Dan Bramall

Additional pictures by Shutterstock.com

ISBN 978 14451 4978 3
Printed in China

MIX
Paper from
responsible sources
FSC® C104740
FSC
www.fsc.org

Franklin Watts
An imprint of
Hachette Children's Group
Part of The Watts Publishing Group
Carmelite House
50 Victoria Embankment
London EC4Y 0DZ
An Hachette UK Company
www.hachette.co.uk

www.franklinwatts.co.uk

Mental changes

During puberty, your brain is changing and growing in important ways.

- You may become more passionate about your interests or what you want to be or do.
- You might sometimes feel stressed – and feel that things are changing too fast.
- You may gradually feel more grown up and develop your own views, opinions and ideas. These might be different to those of your parents or carers.

Relationships

Puberty can also change the way you interact with other people.

- You can get 'crushes' or feel attracted to people.
- The changes of puberty can make you feel self-conscious and shy.
- You may want to have a girlfriend or a boyfriend.
- People often get annoyed with, or embarrassed by, their parents.

We're all different

Puberty doesn't follow a strict timetable – and changes happen at different times for different people. Some people might worry that they are being left behind, while others may feel self-conscious about starting to change before their friends do.

However, it's totally normal for the changes of puberty to happen at a wide range of different ages.

Growing up words

You may hear these words being used to describe you.

Tweenager – someone in between a child and a teenager (usually about ten to 12 years old).

Pubescent – someone in or approaching puberty.

Adolescent – in the stage between childhood and adulthood.

Teenager – someone aged between 13 and 19.

Hormones

As you go through puberty, you'll almost certainly hear someone say 'It's your hormones!' But what does that mean?

What are hormones?

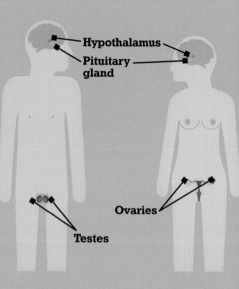

Hormones are body chemicals that make your body work in certain ways. They are released into the bloodstream by several small organs called endocrine glands. Puberty is controlled by the sex hormones released by endocrine glands in your brain (the hypothalamus and pituitary gland) and in your sex organs. These are the ovaries, which only girls have, and the testes or testicles, which only boys have (see page 7 for more on this).

Hypothalamus

Pituitary gland

Ovaries

Testes

Everyday hormones

Hormones aren't just important during puberty – they do all kinds of other jobs too. For example, when you are scared or excited, your body releases the hormone adrenaline. It makes your heart beat faster, so you are ready for quick action. This helps you make quick decisions, or run fast when you are in danger.

After eating, your body releases a hormone called insulin, to help turn sugar in food into energy.

Hormones and puberty

When your body is ready to begin puberty, the pituitary gland, located at the base of the brain (see diagram left), begins to release hormones that travel to the ovaries or the testes. The ovaries release the female sex hormone oestrogen and the testes release the male sex hormone testosterone. These hormones make your body grow in certain ways, make hair grow where it didn't before, and so on.

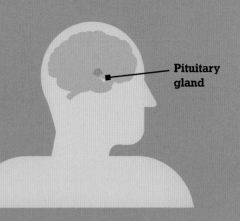

Pituitary gland

The reason this happens is to turn you into an adult, so that you can have children of your own. Of course, you may not want to have children, and that will be your choice. But your body makes the changes anyway.

Like all living things, humans develop the ability to reproduce, or have young.

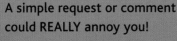

This is why a big part of puberty involves changes to your reproductive system – the body parts used for making and having babies.

Hormones and moods

Puberty hormones often affect your brain as well as your body. Sometimes they can cause intense moods and mood swings.

One minute you'll feel excited or dreamy, the next you might feel grumpy or miserable.

A simple request or comment could REALLY annoy you!

If you have a crush on someone or fall out with a friend, your emotions can feel overwhelming.

Body changes: girls

Boys and girls have different bodies, and puberty changes them even more.

Becoming a woman

During puberty, a girl's body becomes an adult female body. The changes mainly happen in order to allow the woman to get pregnant, carry a baby inside her, give birth and breastfeed – if she chooses to do these things. They affect many parts of the body.

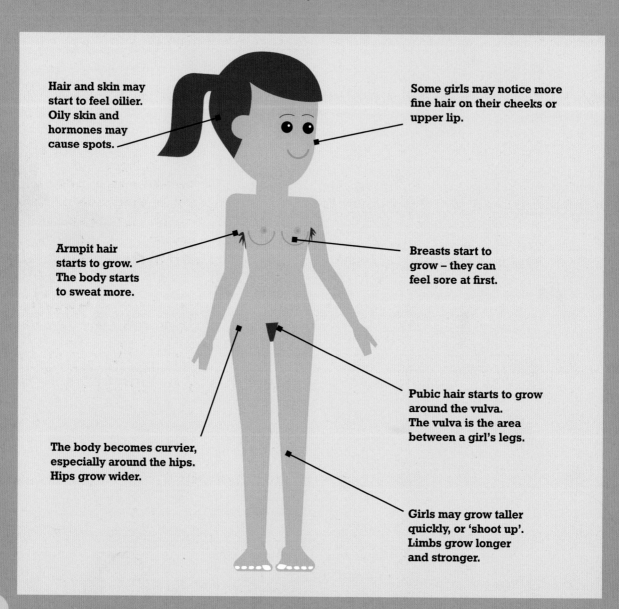

Hair and skin may start to feel oilier. Oily skin and hormones may cause spots.

Some girls may notice more fine hair on their cheeks or upper lip.

Armpit hair starts to grow. The body starts to sweat more.

Breasts start to grow – they can feel sore at first.

The body becomes curvier, especially around the hips. Hips grow wider.

Pubic hair starts to grow around the vulva. The vulva is the area between a girl's legs.

Girls may grow taller quickly, or 'shoot up'. Limbs grow longer and stronger.

What's happening inside?

You can't see all the changes that happen to a girl's body during puberty because some of them are hidden inside. In this picture you can get a better look at the parts inside the female body, known as the reproductive system.

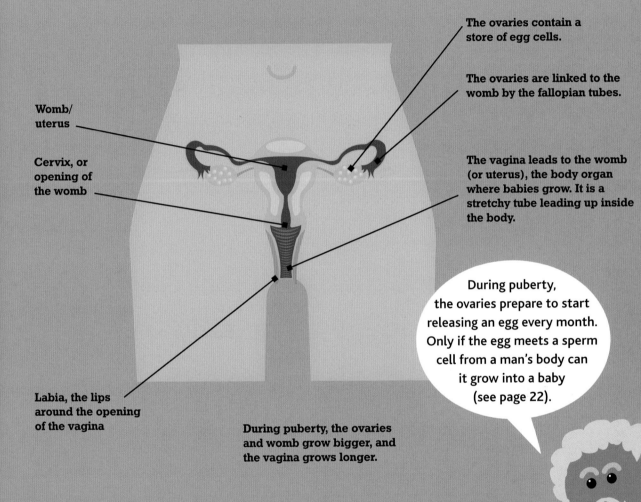

The ovaries contain a store of egg cells.

The ovaries are linked to the womb by the fallopian tubes.

Womb/ uterus

Cervix, or opening of the womb

The vagina leads to the womb (or uterus), the body organ where babies grow. It is a stretchy tube leading up inside the body.

During puberty, the ovaries prepare to start releasing an egg every month. Only if the egg meets a sperm cell from a man's body can it grow into a baby (see page 22).

Labia, the lips around the opening of the vagina

During puberty, the ovaries and womb grow bigger, and the vagina grows longer.

Periods

During puberty girls also start having periods. On average, periods start at around the age of 11 or 12, but they can start any time between eight and 15. About once a month, the womb builds a special lining where an egg could start to grow if the woman became pregnant. If it's not needed, the lining breaks down and comes out of the vagina as a small flow of blood. There's more about periods and pregnancy on page 14.

Body changes: boys

As boys go through puberty their bodies tend to grow bigger and stronger, and several other changes happen too.

Becoming a man

The changes of puberty turn a boy into an adult man. As with girls, many of these changes happen so that men can become fathers (if they want to).

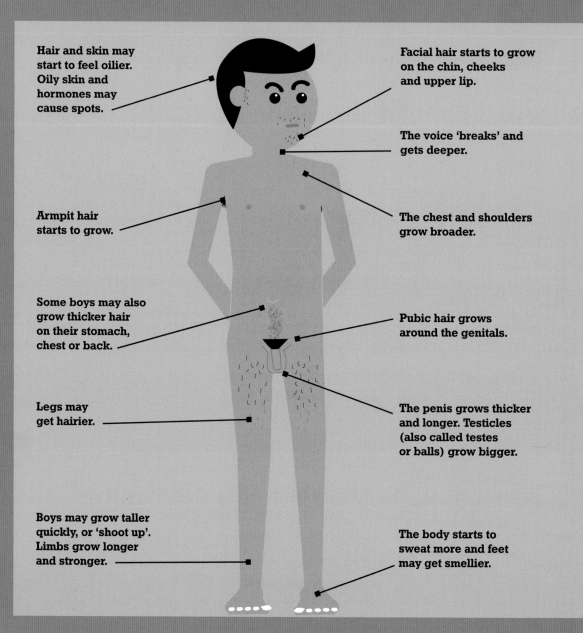

Hair and skin may start to feel oilier. Oily skin and hormones may cause spots.

Facial hair starts to grow on the chin, cheeks and upper lip.

The voice 'breaks' and gets deeper.

Armpit hair starts to grow.

The chest and shoulders grow broader.

Some boys may also grow thicker hair on their stomach, chest or back.

Pubic hair grows around the genitals.

Legs may get hairier.

The penis grows thicker and longer. Testicles (also called testes or balls) grow bigger.

Boys may grow taller quickly, or 'shoot up'. Limbs grow longer and stronger.

The body starts to sweat more and feet may get smellier.

Look inside

A man's reproductive system includes the testicles and penis, and a set of tubes that link them inside the body.

The testicles are where the body makes sperm – special cells used for making babies. To make a baby, a sperm cell has to meet an egg cell from a woman's body. This may happen when people have sex (see page 22). During sex, semen, a liquid containing sperm, comes out of the man's penis.

Urine (or wee) also comes out of a man's body through the urethra and penis – but urine and sperm don't both come out at the same time.

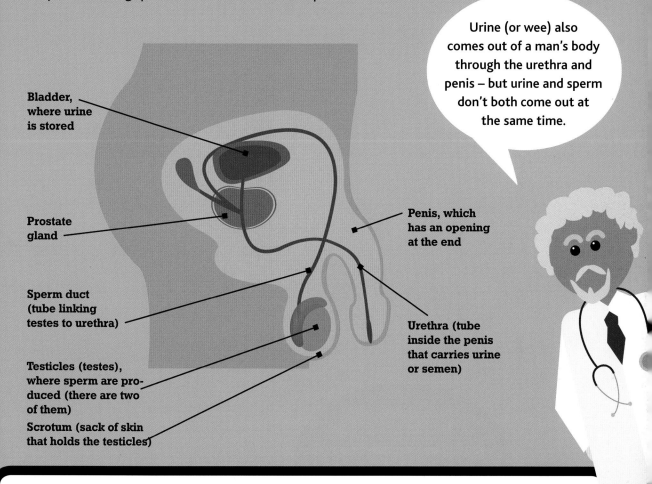

Bladder, where urine is stored

Prostate gland

Sperm duct (tube linking testes to urethra)

Testicles (testes), where sperm are pro-duced (there are two of them)

Scrotum (sack of skin that holds the testicles)

Penis, which has an opening at the end

Urethra (tube inside the penis that carries urine or semen)

Circumcision

Penises can look quite different from each other. Naturally, a penis has a kind of hood over the end, called a foreskin. On a circumcised penis, the foreskin has been removed. Circumcision usually happens when boys are babies and can be done for either health or religious reasons. But whether a man is circumcised or not, his penis will work in exactly the same way.

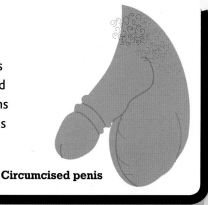

Circumcised penis

Puberty and hair

For both boys and girls, one of the biggest changes during puberty is the growth of new or thicker hair, often in places where there wasn't any before.

What's it for?

Humans evolved from ape-like ancestors that had thick hair all over their bodies, like chimpanzees do.

Today, we are still covered in about five million hairs, but most of them are very short and fine, especially on women's bodies. We only have longer hair in a few places.

On the head – for warmth and protection from the Sun.

Eyebrows and eyelashes – to guard the eyes against rain, sweat and dirt.

Growing new hair

During puberty, boys and girls grow pubic hair around their genitals, as well as armpit hair.

Experts aren't sure exactly why we have hair here – but there are several theories. It's thought to protect and cushion sensitive areas, reduce friction where the legs and arms join the body or help to carry sweat away from the skin.

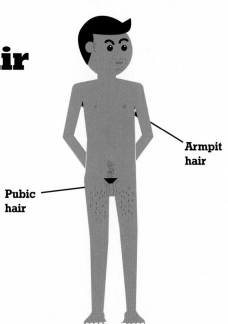

Armpit hair

Pubic hair

Facial hair

Men grow facial hair too, also called a beard and a moustache. Scientists think this doesn't do anything especially useful for the body. Instead, it's thought to be a way of showing that a man is a strong, full-grown adult to help him attract a partner.

More or less hair

There's a huge range of patterns, amounts and types of body hair. Some people are much hairier than others, but variations like these are normal and healthy.

Society and hair

Hair can be very important to people. People often want thick, shiny hair on their head – but choose to remove some of their body hair. This can be partly because of images in magazines and adverts giving people an idea of what a 'perfect' body should look like.

In fact though, humans have been removing body hair for thousands of years, and it has gone through many different fashions over time.

Men often shave off or shape their facial hair.

Women sometimes remove fine hair from their face, or shape their eyebrows, by plucking, waxing or threading.

Leg hair can be waxed or shaved off.

Some people remove their armpit hair and some, or all, of their pubic hair.

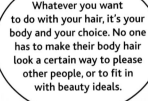

Whatever you want to do with your hair, it's your body and your choice. No one has to make their body hair look a certain way to please other people, or to fit in with beauty ideals.

Take care!

If you do want to shave or remove body or facial hair, be careful! It can be tricky, painful or unsafe if you aren't sure how to use things like razors or wax strips. It's a bad idea for women or girls to shave their face as it can create problems with bristly regrowth. Whether you are male or female, it's best to ask a parent or maybe an older sibling to help you or give you some tips.

Periods

For a girl, starting periods is one of the main changes that happens during puberty. But although it's girls who have periods, it's helpful for everyone to understand what they are.

Why periods happen

Periods occur roughly once a month. Each month, a woman's womb and ovaries go through a series of changes, called the menstrual cycle.

If the egg has not joined with a sperm, the next period will occur on about day 28, and you are back to the beginning of the menstrual cycle (see picture 1).

1

4

Egg

2

3

Egg

1. The start of the period is known as day one. The womb lining breaks down and flows out of the vagina as blood. This is called having a period, or menstruating.

4. The egg reaches the womb. If the egg has joined with a sperm cell, it may implant in the womb lining to grow into a baby.

2. After about 5–7 days, the period ends and the womb lining builds up again. Inside the ovaries, eggs are ripening.

3. At about day 14, one of the ovaries releases an egg – this is called ovulation. It travels towards the womb (also called the uterus).

Periods and pregnancy

Once a girl starts having periods, it means she can get pregnant. Pregnancy happens when an egg released from an ovary joins with a male sperm cell. Sperm cells can get into a girl's or woman's body during sex (see page 22).

This is partly why, in many countries, there are laws against young people having sex until they are about 16 or 17.

Periods usually begin at around the age of 11 or 12 – so it's possible to get pregnant from a young age. But it's not good for a girl's body to have a baby this young, and it will interrupt her education.

What are periods like?

During a period, only a small amount of blood comes out – about 2–3 tablespoons. It flows out very slowly, not all at once.
A period can take from two to seven days, and can vary a lot from person to person, or from month to month. They can be heavier, lighter, closer together or further apart. If you are worried about your periods, visit your doctor.

Thanks to menstruation hormones, many girls and women feel stressed or irritable just before their period, and get period pains, like a stomach ache, in the womb area. This is known as PMT or PMS (Pre-Menstrual Tension, or Syndrome).

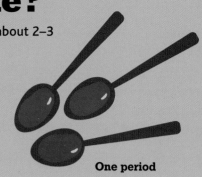

One period

Around ovulation, though, they may feel happy, energetic or creative.

Dealing with periods

Girls and women can use a range of products to catch the blood that flows out of the vagina during a period.

Pads fit inside the knickers and soak up the blood. Pads can be disposable, or washable and re-usable.

Tampons fit inside the vagina to soak up blood.

A menstrual cup is a rubber cup that fits inside the vagina and collects blood. It can be washed out and used again.

Losing blood

Adverts for sanitary products never show real blood! Instead they usually show the product soaking up a blue liquid. Because of this, girls are sometimes shocked to find a period involves bright red blood.

By the time you're ten or 11, you'll already have grown a lot since you were a baby. But during puberty, you can expect to grow faster than ever before in your life.

Growth spurts

A growth spurt is when you grow a lot in a short space of time. They are common in childhood, especially in toddlers. During puberty, most people have a major growth spurt. Some grow as much as 10 cm in just one year.

Since your feet and legs are growing fast, you'll grow out of your shoes and trousers all the time!

Girls and boys

Puberty growth spurts usually happen a bit earlier in girls, and a bit later in boys.

Growth spurt in girls: around ages eight to 13 15

Growth spurt in boys: around ages ten to

HEIGHT (in cm)

HEIGHT (in cm)

180 170 160 150 140 130 120

180 170 160 150 140 130 120

AGE 18   16   14   12   10   8   8   10   12   14   16   18 AGE

Compare these average heights of girls and boys as they grow through puberty.

In a class of ten- or 11-year-olds, the girls are often taller than the boys. Then, by the time they are teenagers, the boys tend to catch up and overtake the girls.

Different heights

How tall a person grows is partly decided by their genes – instructions inside their cells passed on to them from their parents. So if you have tall parents, you're likely to be quite tall too. On average, men grow taller than women – and this is also decided by inherited genes. However, there is a wide range of healthy human heights – and it's normal for some women to be taller than some men.

Worrying about growing

Teenagers sometimes worry that they aren't growing enough, or are being left behind while friends grow taller. Meanwhile, those who are tall may feel self-conscious about that. It doesn't help that short and tall people are often teased about their height.

It's hard to do anything much about how tall you're going to grow, apart from making sure you eat well (see box below). But remember that it really doesn't matter. People of all heights can have successful lives, great jobs and happy relationships.

As with all teasing and bullying, if it's upsetting you, it's important to talk to an adult about it.

When will I reach my full height?

On average, girls reach their adult height at around the age of 15, and boys around 16, but it varies. If you began puberty a little later, you may keep growing later too. Some boys still continue to grow into their early twenties.

These types of foods, minerals and vitamins are thought to help with healthy growth.

Eating for growth

Protein – found in meat, fish, cheese and beans

Calcium – found in dairy foods and green vegetables

Iron – found in meat, eggs and breakfast cereals

Zinc – found in seafood, nuts and seeds

Vitamin C – found in fresh berries, fruit and vegetables

Vitamin D – found in fish and eggs. Also made by the body using sunlight

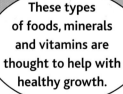

Puberty and skin

Along with all the other changes it brings, puberty can have a big – and often unwelcome – effect on your skin. It may become more oily, sweaty or spotty.

Oily skin

During puberty, your skin often gets oily or greasy, thanks to hormones. Skin naturally produces some oil, but during puberty, it can make too much.

Acne attack!

Oily skin can lead to acne – also known as zits, spots or pimples. It happens when sebum mixes with dead skin cells (which are always flaking off the skin) and blocks a pore. Acne usually affects the face, but it can also appear on the neck, chest, shoulders and back.

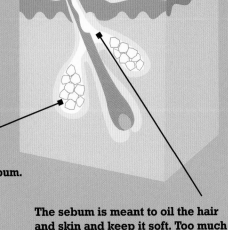

Each hair grows out of a tiny hair follicle, through a hole in the skin called a pore.

Your skin is covered with tiny hairs.

Inside the pore are sebaceous glands. They release an oily substance called sebum.

The sebum is meant to oil the hair and skin and keep it soft. Too much can lead to greasy skin.

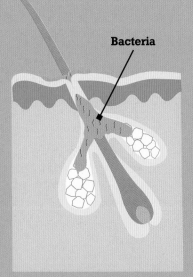

Bacteria

Inside a blocked pore, sebum can build up and become infected with bacteria. The pore may unblock, erupt and heal, or develop a sore, red bump.

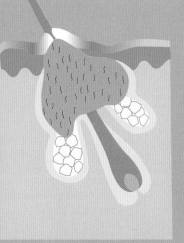

If it forms a sore red bump, it may eventually come to the surface as a zit, sometimes with a white lump of sebum at its centre.

Girls sometimes get acne just before they have a period, due to the hormones involved.

How to help

It's not your fault if you get acne, but there are a few things that can help reduce and prevent it.

Keep skin clean. Wash with warm water twice a day. You can use special anti-acne face wash too.

Avoid touching your face. This can spread acne bacteria around.

Don't pick and squeeze! It's tempting, but this can make zits worse and cause scars.

Keep your hair off your face. Hair also has oil on it and it can transfer onto your face.

Bad acne can make people really miserable and self-conscious. If you feel like this, you don't have to put up with it. It's OK to see a doctor about acne, especially if it's severe.

> There are medicines that can fix most cases of acne.

Stinky sweat

All sweat will smell if it's not washed away as bacteria will grow, causing a 'sweaty' smell. During puberty, glands start to produce a second, thicker type of sweat – which releases a stronger smell if it isn't washed away. So, during puberty, most people start making sure they have a bath or shower every day. You might also want to use a deodorant or anti-perspirant.

> It's best to wash your socks every day, too!

While you go through puberty, something strange is happening to your brain. This can affect your feelings, moods and behaviour.

In your brain

The brain is made up of billions of brain cells. Each one is like a tiny tree, with many branches that reach out and connect to other brain cells. These connections make complex pathways through your brain. When you think, signals zoom around your brain along these pathways.

As you experience and remember things, your brain cells make more connections. You learn a lot during childhood, so by 11 or 12 you have a huge number of connections.

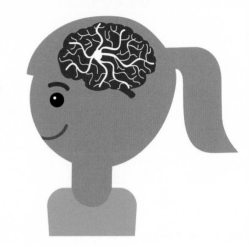

Teenage changes

At around the age of 13, though, things start to change. The brain starts to remove or 'prune' away connections, while making others stronger. It's basically 'fixing' itself into a more permanent pattern, ready for adulthood.

Brain connections at different stages

At birth

At the age of seven – lots of connections

At the age of 15 – fewer, stronger connections

Up and down

During this time, the changes in the brain, along with puberty hormones, can make you feel as if you're on a mood rollercoaster.

EXCITED
EXHAUSTED
JEALOUS
IN LOVE
CONFUSED
WORRIED
SAD
HAPPY
GRUMPY

Stressy situations

On top of this, teenagers are often going through things that can add to their worry and stress. Things like...

Relationship issues

Exams

Friendship issues

Worrying about appearance, or the changes of puberty

Bullying

Parents separating

Feeling stressed can make you tense, anxious, teary, tired or even ill. But there are quite a few stress-busting solutions you can try...

Distract yourself
Read, play music, see a film. Focusing on something else gives your brain a break.

Laugh and have fun
Chat and joke with friends, and do things you enjoy.

Exercise
Take any kind of exercise – sport, dance, walking the dog. It is great for releasing stress.

Sleep well
Turn off your phone and your computer and go to sleep. Not getting enough sleep adds to stress levels. Lie in when you can!

Eat well
Make sure you eat when you're hungry and eat a wide range of foods you enjoy. They will feed your brain and help you calm down.

Talk it over
Talk through your worries with a trusted friend, parent or teacher – it can make them seem less overwhelming.

Soooooo embarrassing!

It's totally normal to feel this way!

One of the strong feelings people experience during puberty is embarrassment! Parents' actions can make you want the ground to swallow you up. You might feel horribly awkward around someone you have a crush on, or if anyone laughs at you.

Sex and sexuality

In nature, sex exists in order to make babies. But people also behave in a sexual way because they enjoy it, and it can be a way of expressing love and closeness.

How sex works

In sex between a man and a woman, the man's penis fits into the woman's vagina. Semen containing sperm comes out of the penis and up into the womb and fallopian tubes. There, an egg and sperm cell can meet, join and become a cell that can grow into a baby.

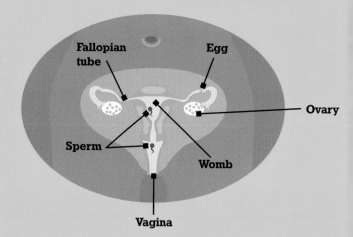

Fallopian tube

Egg

Ovary

Sperm

Womb

Vagina

Sexual feelings

During puberty, the body prepares to be able to have sex. The genitals develop and many people begin to have sexual feelings, or feel 'turned on'. When boys feel turned on, their penis gets hard and sticks out, known as an erection. Girls can have similar feelings, but it's not so easy to see.

Masturbation is when a person touches or rubs their own genitals because it feels nice. This can lead to an intense sexual feeling called an orgasm, or 'coming'. Masturbating isn't bad for you – and most people do it. It's a normal part of growing up.

Do NOT Disturb

However, things like sexual feelings, genitals and masturbation are private. Although they are normal and nothing to be ashamed of, they are considered rude if they are made public.

Ejaculation

During an orgasm, semen containing sperm comes out of a boy's or man's penis. This is called ejaculation. It sometimes happens at night during sleep, and then it's called a 'wet dream'. If this happens to you, just reach for a tissue and mop yourself up. It can be embarrassing, but it's normal and natural.

Attraction

As well as sexual feelings, you may start to have romantic feelings – feelings that you fancy or love someone, are attracted to them, or have a 'crush' on them.

You can't wait to see them or be near them... but when you are, you may feel tongue-tied and awkward. Maybe you think about kissing them... or would like them to be your boyfriend or girlfriend.

This is normal too. During puberty, people often do start having relationships, kissing and sometimes exploring each other's bodies.

Actually having sex, though, is a big step, and it's important to wait until you're ready.

Sex is against the law until you are 16, or around that age (depending on which country you're in). Even then, you don't have to have sex until you want to – and many people wait until they are older.

Many people have these feelings during puberty, but not everyone. You're also normal if you don't!

Sexual preference

Most people are heterosexual, and are attracted to the opposite sex – boys are attracted to girls and girls are attracted to boys. Some feel attracted to their own sex, which is called being homosexual – or gay or lesbian (for gay women). And some are attracted to both sexes (known as being bisexual), or none. Your sexual preference is known as your 'sexuality'.

Under pressure

During puberty, people often begin to care more than ever about what friends and classmates think of them. It can feel as if there's a lot of pressure to fit in or do what other people want.

Peer pressure

Your peers are people around the same age as you – friends, schoolmates or siblings. Peer pressure means expectations or persuasion from your peers that can influence what you do.

Lots of things are affected by peer pressure. They include everyday things such as what you wear or what bands you listen to.

They can also include more serious things like whether to try smoking, drinking or drugs, or decisions to do with relationships and sex.

Often people can be teased, excluded, laughed at or have rumours spread about them by their peers, especially if they don't 'fit in'.

It's up to you

It can be very difficult to resist peer pressure, because no one wants to be teased, laughed at or called names. Teenagers often want to be seen as cool by their peers. But it's important to remember that you are the person your decisions will affect, and you have every right to make your own choices and be proud of them.

Pressure in relationships

When people begin having relationships, or start becoming interested in sex, that can lead to pressure, too. Sometimes, one person wants to do more sexual things than the other is comfortable with. Or there can be pressure at school to take part in things like sharing pictures of your body on your phone, with people calling you boring or a scaredy-cat if you don't.

When it comes to sexual things, you are in charge of your own body, and you get to decide. It is OK to say no.

Sexual respect

It's not OK for anyone to touch or talk to another person in a sexual way, unless the other person consents, or agrees. Doing this can count as sexual harassment or indecent assault, which are against the law.

It is also never OK to pressure, coerce or force someone into doing anything sexual. Forcing someone to have sex is a serious crime known as rape.

If someone does treat you like this against your wishes, it's best to tell a person you can trust about it as soon as possible.

Privacy

During puberty, many people start to want more privacy and personal space. You may want to lock the bathroom, keep the bedroom door shut when you're getting changed, or ask family members to knock before coming into your room. The same is true at school, sports clubs or out and about – you are entitled to privacy and other people should respect what you want.

Keep Out!

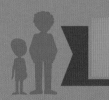 

An adult for life

Puberty is about becoming who you're going to be for most of your life – a grown-up version of yourself! That's a good thing, because as an adult, you'll have the freedom to do and be whatever you want.

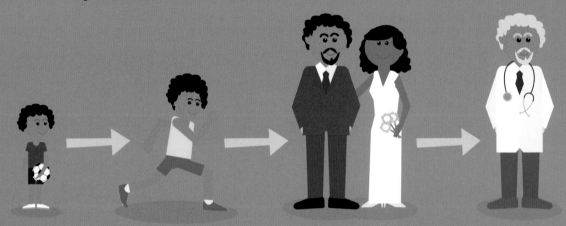

A long journey

Puberty involves many different kinds of changes, strong emotions, and ups and downs. It can be alarming or stressful at times. And it goes on for several years, which can feel like forever.

But your body and brain need that time to adjust, grow and prepare for the next stage of your life. It would probably be even more alarming to wake up one day and find you had become an adult overnight!

Lots to look forward to

As teenagers approach adulthood at around the age of 17 or 18, they often find things improve a lot, and they feel calmer and happier.

Emotions may start to calm down and not feel so overwhelming.

School bullies or pressure from schoolmates can be left behind as school comes to an end.

You may become closer again to parents who seemed so annoying and embarrassing before.

You may feel more confident in who you are, and happy in your own skin.

People who have suffered from oily skin and zits often find they start to clear up.

Young adults start to feel ready for the big changes and responsibilities ahead – like going travelling, starting work, going away to college or leaving home.

Healthy for life

Puberty presents you with lots of new challenges and things to learn, such as how to look after your changing body, have healthy, respectful relationships and resist pressure. It's not always easy. But those habits and skills will stand you in good stead for a lifetime of being a happy, healthy adult. And as your life goes on, you'll continue to change, grow and enjoy new experiences and adventures.

Once puberty is over, you'll almost certainly be living in your new, adult body for many decades to come. Look after it now, and it will look after you!

What happens when?

Check out these charts – one for girls and one for boys – for an at-a-glance guide to when you can expect the changes of puberty to happen. These charts show the most likely times for most people to experience these things, but changes can sometimes happen earlier or later too.

Girls

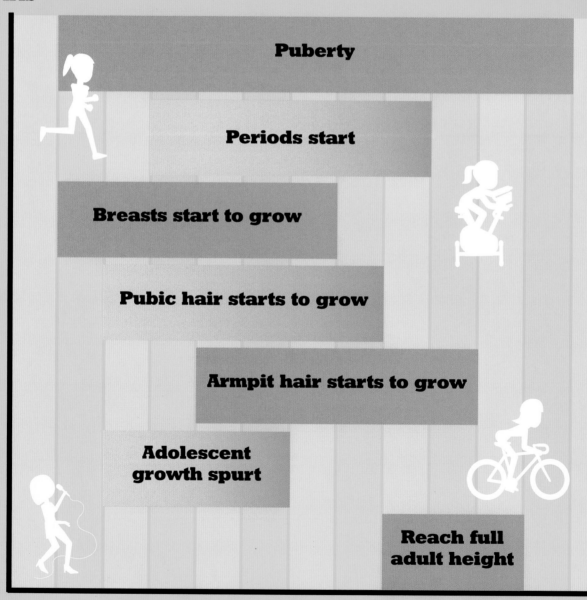

Puberty

Periods start

Breasts start to grow

Pubic hair starts to grow

Armpit hair starts to grow

Adolescent growth spurt

Reach full adult height

Age 7 8 9 10 11 12 13 14 15 16 17 18

Puberty

Pubic hair
starts to grow

Armpit hair
starts to grow

Voice breaks
(or gets deeper)

Penis and testes
grow bigger

Facial hair
starts to grow

Adolescent
growth spurt

Reach full
adult height

Age 7 8 9 10 11 12 13 14 15 16 17 18 19 20

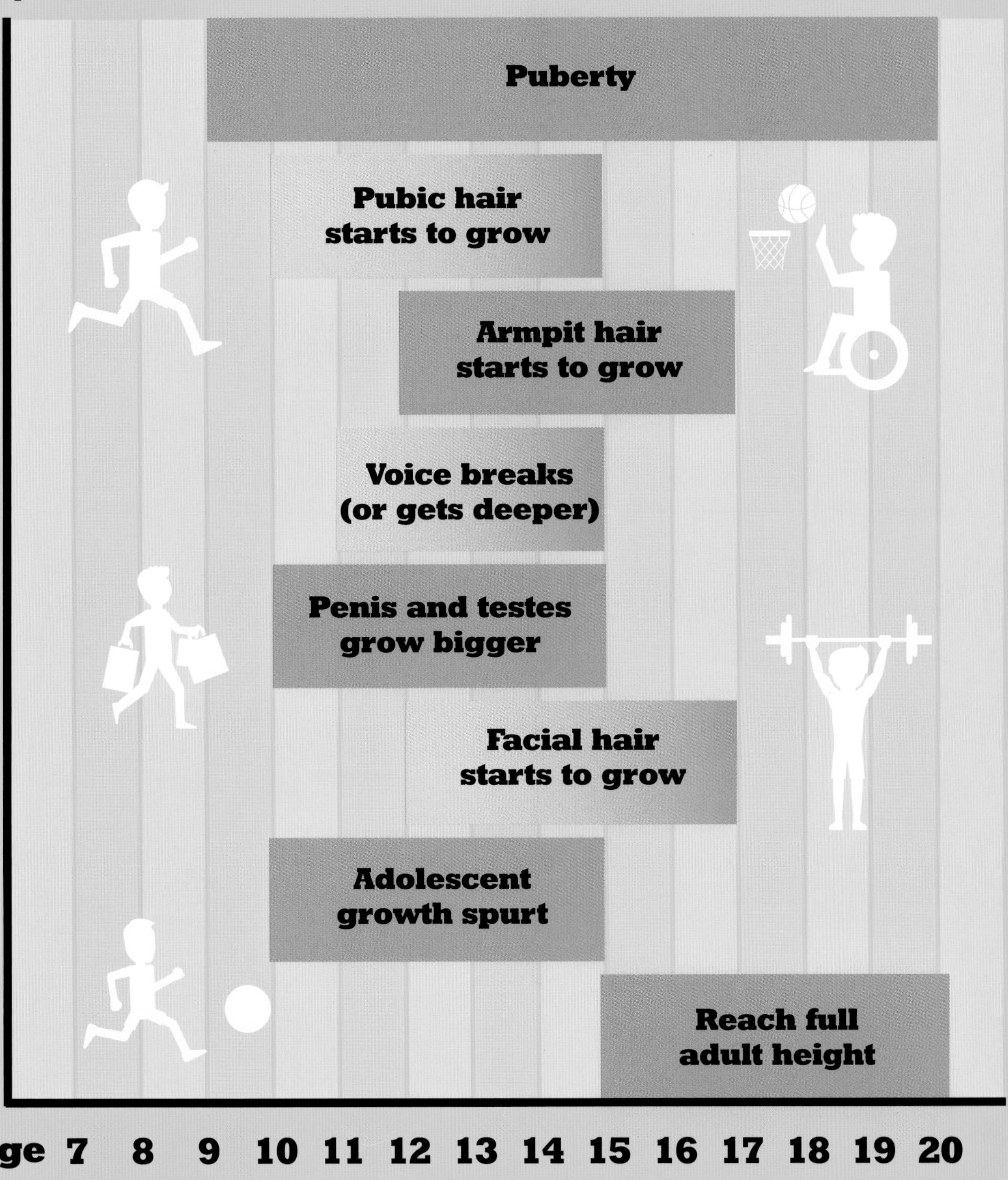

If you're worried that any changes are happening to you unusually early or late, you can visit your doctor for advice.

Glossary

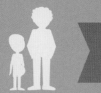

acne Spots (or 'zits') on the face, neck, chest or back, often appearing during puberty.

bisexual Sexually attracted to both your own and the opposite sex.

circumcise To remove the foreskin from the penis.

coming Another word for having an orgasm.

crush A strong feeling of love or sexual attraction for another person.

egg A sex cell released from a woman's ovaries, which can grow into a baby if it combines with a sperm cell.

ejaculation This happens when semen comes out of the penis, usually during an orgasm.

erection This happens when a boy or man feels turned on and his penis becomes stiff.

fallopian tubes Tubes inside a girl's or woman's body that link the ovaries to the womb.

foreskin A hood of skin that covers the end of the penis.

gay Another word for homosexual.

genes Information stored inside body cells that tells the body how to work and grow.

genitals Sex organs that can be seen on the outside of the body.

growth spurt A period of extra-fast growth in height.

heterosexual Being sexually attracted to the opposite sex from yourself.

homosexual Being sexually attracted to the same sex as yourself.

hormones Chemicals your body releases to make some body parts work, grow or change.

lesbian A name for a female homosexual.

masturbation Touching or rubbing your own genitals because it feels good.

mental To do with the mind.

orgasm An intense sexual feeling in the genitals.

ovaries Two organs inside a woman's body that release egg cells.

peer pressure Pressure from your peers (friends, schoolmates or people a similar age to you) to behave in particular ways.

period A flow of blood and womb lining from the vagina, roughly once a month.

physical To do with the body.

PMT or PMS Pre-Menstrual Tension or Syndrome Feeling stressed and irritable just before a period.

pregnant Having a baby growing inside the womb.

pubic hair Hair that grows around the genitals from puberty onwards.

rape Forcing another person to have sex, which is a serious crime.

scrotum The bag of thin skin surrounding the testes.

semen The liquid that surrounds sperm cells as they leave the penis.

sexuality A person's sexual preferences, or the things that turn them on.

sperm A sex cell released from a man's testes, which may grow into a baby if it combines with an egg cell.

stress Mental or emotional tension or

exhaustion.

testes Two male organs below the penis that produce sperm; also called balls.

testicles Another name for testes or balls.

urine The scientific name for wee.

uterus Another name for the womb.

vagina The tube in a woman's or girl's body leading from the vulva to the womb.

vulva A woman's or girl's genitals, the sex organs that can be seen on the outside of the body.

wet dream This happens when a boy or man has an orgasm and ejaculates while asleep.

womb The organ inside a woman's body where a baby can live and grow before birth.

Further information

Books

The Boys' Guide to Growing Up
by Phil Wilkinson, Wayland, 2017

The Girls' Guide to Growing Up
by Anita Naik, Wayland, 2017

Dr Christian's Guide to Growing Up
by Dr Christian Jessen, Scholastic, 2013

Websites

Kidshealth: Puberty
http://www.cyh.com/HealthTopics/
HealthTopicDetailsKids.
aspx?p=335&np=289&id=1774

4You – Online leaflet about puberty
http://www.nhs.uk/Livewell/puberty/
Documents/4youmarch2010nonprinting.pdf

Puberty 101
http://puberty101.com

NOTE TO PARENTS AND TEACHERS:
Every effort has been made by the Publishers to ensure that these websites are suitable for children, that they are of the highest educational value, and that they contain no inappropriate or offensive material. However, because of the nature of the Internet, it is impossible to guarantee that the contents of these sites will not be altered. We strongly advise that Internet access is supervised by a responsible adult.

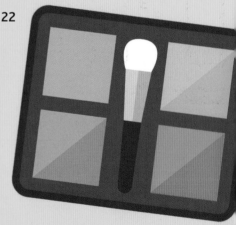